Donated to
the Stratham Memorial School
Library
by:
Libby Abizaid
On the occasion of
her 9th Birthday
on October 1, 2004

DK DORLING KINDERSLEY *READERS*

Level 2

Level 3

Level 4

A Note to Parents

Dorling Kindersley Readers is a compelling new program for beginning readers, designed in conjunction with leading literacy experts, including Dr. Linda Gambrell, President of the National Reading Conference and past board member of the International Reading Association.

Beautiful illustrations and superb full-color photographs combine with engaging, easy-to-read stories to offer a fresh approach to each subject in the series. Each *Dorling Kindersley Reader* is guaranteed to capture a child's interest while developing his or her reading skills, general knowledge, and love of reading.

The four levels of *Dorling Kindersley Readers* are aimed at different reading abilities, enabling you to choose the books that are exactly right for your child:

Level 1 – Beginning to read
Level 2 – Beginning to read alone
Level 3 – Reading alone
Level 4 – Proficient readers

The "normal" age at which a child begins to read can be anywhere from three to eight years old, so these levels are intended only as a general guideline.

No matter which level you select, you can be sure that you are helping your child learn to read, then read to learn!

Dorling **DK** Kindersley

LONDON, NEW YORK, SYDNEY, DELHI, PARIS,
MUNICH and JOHANNESBURG

Project Editor Susan Malyan
Art Editor C. David Gillingwater
Managing Editor Bridget Gibbs
Senior Art Editor Sarah Ponder
Senior DTP Designer Bridget Roseberry
US Editor Regina Kahney
Production Shivani Pandey
Picture Researcher Frances Vargo
Jacket Designer Victoria Harvey
Indexer Lynn Bresler
Illustrator Malcolm Chandler

Reading Consultant
Linda B. Gambrell, Ph.D.

First American Edition 2000
2 4 6 8 10 9 7 5 3 1
Published in the United States by DK Publishing, Inc.
95 Madison Avenue, New York, New York 10016

Published in Great Britain by Dorling Kindersley Limited.

Library of Congress Cataloging-in-Publication Data
Hooper, Meredith.
 Antarctic adventure: exploring the frozen south / by Meredith
Hooper. -- 1st American ed.
  p. cm. -- (Dorling Kindersley readers)
 ISBN 0-7894-6683-X -- ISBN 0-7894-6684-8 (pbk.)
 1. Antarctica--Discovery and exploration--Juvenile literature.
 2. Explorers--Antarctica--Juvenile literature. [1. Antarctica--
Discovery and exploration. 2. Explorers.]
 I. Title. II. Series.
 G863 .H66 2000
 919.8904--dc21
                                          00-027392

Color reproduction by Colourscan, Singapore
Printed and bound in China by L Rex

The publisher would like to thank the following for their
kind permission to reproduce their photographs:

Key: t=top, a=above, b=below, l=left, r=right, c=center

Corbis UK Ltd: 44t, Joel Bennett 34l, 20bl, 40t, Ann Hawthorne 17t, 25t,
Peter Johnson 37t, 39br, Galen Rowell 15t; **Corbis Bettmann:** 12t; **Hulton
Deutsch Collection:** 18t, 32t, 41b; **National Archives:** 41t; **Mary Evans
Picture Library:** 23br; **Mawson Antarctic Collection / The University
of Adelaide:** 24t, 25b; **Borge Ousland:** 46-7; **Oxford Scientific Films:**
Raymond J.C. Cannon 8t; **Popperfoto:** 6t, 11b, 18b; **Royal Geographical
Society:** 35b, Frank Hurley 33r, 34b, 44b; **Frank Spooner Pictures:**
Steve Morgan 4b; **Scott Polar Institute:** 8b, 20t, 22b, 23t, 30t.

Additional photography: National Maritime Museum, Geoff Brightling,
Peter Chadwick, Lynton Gardener, Steve Gorton, Dave King, Karl Shone.

see our complete
catalogue at
www.dk.com

Contents

DK DORLING KINDERSLEY *READERS*

PROFICIENT **4** READERS

ANTARCTIC ADVENTURE

EXPLORING THE FROZEN SOUTH

Written by Meredith Hooper

DK

A Dorling Kindersley Book

Going to Antarctica

Lumps of ice the size of refrigerators bump and roll against the ship's sides. An iceberg looms like a lonely island. Ahead, the pack ice glares white against the gray sky. Somewhere beyond is the ice-covered continent of Antarctica.

Antarctica is the coldest, windiest, highest, driest, quietest, cleanest, loneliest, and emptiest place on Earth. It is so cold that in winter the surface of the sea freezes.

Even in summer, the sea around the continent is strewn with pieces of floating ice.

Today, travelers to Antarctica go in specially strengthened ships called icebreakers. They wear the latest windproof and waterproof clothing.

The men who first explored Antarctica a hundred years ago sailed in wooden ships and tried to keep warm with hand-knitted woollen underwear. They had amazing, terrifying adventures.

You can read their extraordinary stories in this book.

ANTARCTICA

Weddell Sea

Ronne Ice Shelf

Polar Plateau

● South Pole

Transantarctic Mountains

Ross Ice Shelf

Adélie Land

Icy continent
Most of the world's ice is in Antarctica. The land is covered by an enormous ice cap, up to 2½ miles thick.

Antarctic plants
The only plants that can survive in the Antarctic are mosses and lichens. They grow very slowly in the harsh conditions.

The worst journey

Apsley Cherry-Garrard
This young Englishman went to Antarctica in 1911 with an expedition led by Captain Scott. During the first winter, Cherry-Garrard, Dr Bill Wilson, and Birdie Bowers went on an expedition to collect emperor penguin eggs.

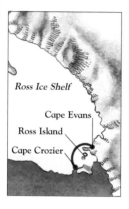

Ross Ice Shelf

Cape Evans

Ross Island

Cape Crozier

Cherry's route
Cherry-Garrard, Wilson, and Bowers set out from the expedition hut at Cape Evans on Ross Island. They walked over the sea ice to the penguin colony at Cape Crozier, on the other side of the island. The 65 mile journey took 23 days.

Cherry-Garrard and his two companions were the first people to travel overland during the Antarctic winter. But after only a few days trekking across the ice, they were in a terrible state.

Frostbite blisters bulged like slugs along Cherry's fingers.

His lips were cracked and raw. His reindeer-skin sleeping bag was frozen stiff into a twisted shape, yet somehow he pushed his weary body inside it once more. Uncontrollable shivering fits seized him, shaking his body like a skeleton in a dance.

The sleeping bag slowly thawed, turning soft and soggy. The blisters on his fingers unfroze, and the pain was agonizing. His clothes were sopping wet.

When morning came, Cherry crawled out of their tent and his wet clothes froze solid. It was -63°F, the middle of winter, and pitch dark.

Clothing
As Cherry sweated, his woollen clothes got wet. They froze when he went outside, then thawed when he was in the warm tent.

Cherry's book
Cherry wrote a book about this expedition. He called it *The Worst Journey in the World.*

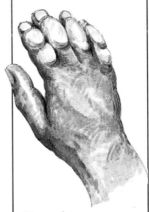

Frostbite
Extreme cold can freeze toes, fingers, and parts of the face. This is called frostbite.

The Antarctic winter
In Antarctica it is very dark in the winter. At Cape Evans, for example, the sun does not rise at all for four months in winter.

Home-made candlestick
Explorers tried to get as much use out of their few supplies as possible. Dr Bill Wilson made this candlestick from an empty biscuit tin.

Cherry, Wilson, and Bowers were trying to collect some emperor penguin eggs to take back to England. Scientists there hoped that by studying these eggs they would learn more about the origin of birds.

At Cape Crozier, the emperor penguins stood in the gloom on the sea ice, huddling tightly together to keep warm. The big birds shuffled awkwardly away, making haunting, high calls as the men groped around, picking up their eggs.

Climbing back across the dangerous ice, Cherry slipped in the dark.

He broke two of their five eggs.

Exhausted, the three men crawled into a little igloo they had built out of rocks and snow blocks, partway up a mountainside.

"Things must improve," said Bill, trying to be cheerful.

But during the night the wind began to blow until it reached blizzard force, thundering and roaring overhead.

Emperor penguins
The female emperor penguin lays one egg in the middle of winter. The male puts the egg on his feet and keeps it warm under a fold of skin. The chick hatches in early spring.

Strong winds
Antarctica is the windiest country on Earth. The dry, cold winds can blow at hurricane speed.

Rock igloo
The men's igloo had rock walls with a sled on top to support the canvas roof. They had to crawl inside on all fours.

Eating snow
The men had no water to drink, so they ate bits of snow instead.

Frozen clothes
When the men finally stumbled back into the expedition hut, their frozen clothes had to be cut off them.

The wind wrenched the canvas roof of their igloo up and down until the canvas split into ragged strips. Rocks started to fall on them from the walls. The men managed to roll their sleeping bags over and lie on their stomachs for protection.

It was July 23, Bill's birthday. What a birthday! "Occasionally I thumped Bill," said Birdie. "As he still moved, I knew he was alive."

Bill Wilson

Every now and then they opened their bags and picked up bits of snow to put into their mouths. Cherry had given up hope. They couldn't survive.

The blizzard screamed and howled for two days. At last it began to ease. Miraculously, they found their tent, which had blown away, and some of their possessions.

Somehow the three men struggled back to the expedition hut, where Scott and their other companions were waiting for them. It was incredible that they had survived. They had even managed to save the penguin eggs, which Cherry took back to England to be studied. ❖

Expedition hut
Explorers in Antarctica usually had a base camp where they kept their equipment and supplies. The men lived there in the expedition hut.

To the Pole
Three months after this expedition, Scott and some of his men set out for the South Pole.

Birdie Bowers

Apsley Cherry-Garrard

Back at the expedition hut, the three exhausted men devoured some food.

11

Capturing the Pole

Roald Amundsen
In 1910, Amundsen set off from Norway in his ship, the *Fram*. He planned to be the first person to reach the South Pole. Amundsen was an experienced explorer who had already spent a lot of time in the Arctic and the Antarctic.

Famous ship
The *Fram* was already famous. She belonged to another explorer, called Nansen, who had used her to cross the Arctic by drifting in the ice.

95...96...97... With a quick grab around the scruff of the neck, the last dog was on board. Now *Fram's* decks were crammed with dogs.

Amundsen gave each of the men 10 dogs to look after on the ship.

They yanked at their chains and growled at one another.

"They're our new shipmates," said Roald Amundsen to his men, "and they come first, all the time."

Amundsen wanted to reach the South Pole, and he intended to be the first person to get there. If he wasn't first, there was no point in trying. The dogs were the most important part of his plans.

But Amundsen had a rival, Captain Robert Scott. Scott had tried to reach the South Pole once before, and Amundsen knew that he was about to try again.

Scott planned to get there using sleds pulled by a mixture of motors, ponies, dogs, and men. Amundsen intended to use just dogs and sleds, the method he had learned from the native people in the Arctic.

Sled dogs
Explorers brought huskies to Antarctica to pull their sleds. Huskies come from the Arctic, where they are used by the native people. They have thick coats and are very strong.

The Pole
The explorer Ernest Shackleton had almost reached the South Pole in 1909. He discovered that the Pole was situated on a high plateau in the middle of Antarctica.

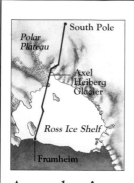

Amundsen's route
Amundsen's base was at Framheim on the Ross Ice Shelf. He climbed up the Axel Heiberg glacier on to the polar plateau.

Arctic clothes
Amundsen's team wore clothes based on the Arctic people's fur anorak.

The *Fram* reached Antarctica in the summer. The men built their base camp, "Framheim," on the ice near the edge of the ocean.

During the winter, the men worked hard to improve their equipment. To reduce weight, they shaved wood off the sleds and skis and repacked their food. A little silk emergency tent was dyed with ink and shoe polish so that it would show up against the snow.

Amundsen couldn't wait to get started. Perhaps Scott was already on his way, using those motorized sleds!

Early in spring, Amundsen set off, but he had to turn back. It was still too cold.

Then on October 20, 1911 he set off again. Amundsen and his four men were on skis, while their five sleds were pulled by 52 of the dogs.

On November 16 they reached gigantic unknown mountains. They set the dogs climbing, up steep passes, up a treacherous glacier, scrabbling and heaving over flint-hard ice, pulling the loaded sleds. People thought that dogs could never climb like this. Amundsen believed they could.

Glacier
A glacier is a slow-moving river of ice. In Antarctica, enormous glaciers force their way from the plateau through the mountains. Their surfaces are cracked with crevasses.

Food depot
Explorers left supplies of food and fuel along their route in stores called depots. On the way back, they used the food and fuel from the depots.

Measuring the distance
A wheel fixed to the back of each sled measured how far they went each day, so Amundsen knew when he had traveled the right distance to reach the Pole.

At last they were on the immense plateau which Amundsen knew stretched all the way to the Pole. They traveled on in thick, driving snow, mist, and deep cold.

Amundsen had nightmares about Scott. Was he ahead? Would the British get there first? Then the sun came out, and one afternoon the dog drivers called, "Halt!"

They had arrived at the South Pole. They looked around, checking for signs of Scott. There were none. "The great thing is that we are here as the first men, no English flag waves," wrote one of the men in his diary.

On December 16, 1911, they put up the dark silk tent and raised the Norwegian flag. Amundsen wrote letters to the king of Norway and Scott, and put them in the tent. They wanted to leave a record of their achievement.

Then they turned and started on their journey home. It was a long way to their hut on the edge of the ocean, but they made it back safely. ❖

The South Pole
Today the South Pole is marked by this small, striped pole. There is a United States scientific station nearby, called Amundsen-Scott Base.

The southern journey

Robert Scott
Captain Scott, a British naval officer, made his first expedition to Antarctica in 1901–04. His second expedition arrived in Antarctica in 1911. Like Amundsen, Scott was determined to be the first man to reach the South Pole.

Scott's route
Scott followed the route discovered by Shackleton. He set out from his base camp at Cape Evans, and climbed up the Beardmore Glacier to reach the polar plateau and the South Pole.

All through the Antarctic winter, Captain Scott worried. How could he carry all the food and fuel he needed for the journey to the South Pole? Were motorized sleds best?

Scott and some of his men in the expedition hut at Cape Evans.

Or should he pull the sleds with ponies, dogs, or men? In the end, he decided to use all of these methods.

Scott's expedition started out on October 24, 1911. The two motorized sleds quickly broke down. The ponies struggled in the snow and had to be shot. At the mountains, they sent the dogs back.

Now the men had to drag the sleds up a glacier and onto the

polar plateau. It was exhausting work. But Scott had always planned that his men would haul their sleds.

On January 3, 1912, Scott chose four men to join him on the final part of the journey. He was still 173 miles from the South Pole.

Motorized sled
This cigarette card shows one of Scott's motorized sleds. It was the first vehicle with tracks designed to run on snow.

Bowers and Wilson
Among Scott's men who went to the Pole were Wilson and Bowers. They had been on the earlier expedition with Cherry-Garrard.

Too late
By the time Scott started the final part of his journey, Amundsen was halfway home.

Scott and his four companions arrived at the South Pole on January 17, 1912. They stared bitterly at the Norwegian flag. The worst had happened. They had been beaten by Amundsen.

They took some photographs and ate a meager meal with frostbitten fingers. The South Pole seemed an awful place.

Compasses
Scott's men used these compasses in the Antarctic. The small one shows direction. The bigger one was used to plot their position, using the sun.

This photo shows Scott and his men at the South Pole. Oates, Scott, and Evans are standing at the back. Bowers and Wilson are sitting in front.

The return journey would be a
desperate struggle. The days were
getting colder. They were exhausted
and hungry, and there wasn't
enough food in the depots on the
route back. They had no margin for
any delay – for bad weather, illness,
injury, or getting lost. Dragging the
heavy sled was an awful labor.

They went back across the polar
plateau to the mountains, and down
the glacier. At the bottom of the
glacier Evans collapsed and died.

Sledding food
Scott took
special rations
on his journey:
cocoa, sugar,
biscuits, butter,
tea, and a kind
of dried meat
mixture called
pemmican.

Man-hauling
Scott's men
harnessed
themselves to
their sleds and
dragged them
along. This
method, called
man-hauling,
was slow and
exhausting.

A month later, Laurence Oates knew that he could not keep going. He was suffering great pain. His foot was frostbitten. One morning, he limped out of the tent, where they had spent the night, to die outside.

Scott struggled on for a few more days with Birdie Bowers and Bill Wilson. They camped perhaps a day's march from a big depot of food.

Next day a blizzard began. They could not travel. They were hungry and weak.

The blizzard blew the next day, and the next.

One by one, the men died in their sleeping bags, in the cold and the icy silence. Snow covered the tent. Winter came, and darkness.

In early summer, a search party saw the top of a tent sticking out of the snow. They dug down and discovered the bodies, the men's diaries, and their last letters to their families.

They made a cross out of skis and left the bodies where they had found them. ❖

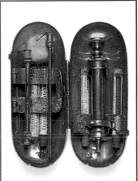

Medical kit
Polar explorers carried a small medical kit like this one. It contained drugs for treating injuries and frostbite.

Monument
The search party built this snow monument to mark the spot where Scott, Wilson, and Bowers died.

The incredible journey

Douglas Mawson
The Australian geologist Douglas Mawson first traveled to Antarctica in 1907 on an expedition led by Ernest Shackleton. In 1911, at age 29, Mawson led an expedition to explore the area of Antarctica called Adélie Land.

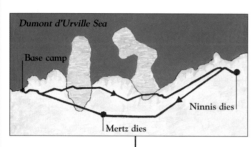

Dumont d'Urville Sea
Base camp
Ninnis dies
Mertz dies

Mawson's route
Mawson sailed south from Australia and landed on the coast of Adélie Land. In November 1912 parties of men set off from the expedition's base to explore the coast. Mawson, Mertz, and Ninnis traveled east.

"Watch it!" Douglas Mawson glanced back at the sled behind. He was crossing a crevasse and called out a warning.

Mawson and his companions, Ninnis and Mertz, had already crossed hundreds of these deep splits in the ice on this expedition. They had been exploring for six weeks, working their way over one glacier after another.

Some crevasses gaped open. Others, like this one, lay hidden under a bridge of snow. The snow bridge seemed thick. But crevasses were always dangerous.

Suddenly, the snow bridge collapsed and Ninnis fell into the depths of the crevasse. The six best sled dogs – plus the sled carrying their tent and most of the food – fell with him. All gone.

Horrified, Mawson peered down into the hole. All the dog food had fallen into the crevasse. The six remaining dogs had nothing to eat. Now he and Xavier Mertz, the survivors, somehow had to get back to their base hut on the coast.

Crevasse
A crevasse is a deep crack in the ice. It is formed when glacier ice flows over hidden rocks, or down a slope, and splits apart. A crevasse can be up to 100 ft wide.

Mawson's companions, Mertz and Ninnis, set out with heavily laden sleds.

They tried to keep the dogs alive, but as each one weakened it was killed and eaten by the two men and the remaining dogs.

Then Mertz became ill. Mawson thought that he was suffering from hunger and the cold. At last, Mertz was too ill to walk.

Explorer's sled
Mawson took three sleds, loaded with 1,530 lbs of equipment, food, and fuel. The main sled was 11 ft long.

Christmas dinner
On Christmas Day 1912, Mawson and Mertz ate a stew of dog bones and two scraps of biscuit.

Mawson tried pulling him on the sled, trudging short distances at a time. But the next night Mertz died, and Mawson was alone.

Mawson lay in the shelter they'd made from a tent cover over skis.

He was desperately hungry and weak, suffering from the same awful symptoms as Mertz. His skin was falling off. His hair had turned gray and was dropping out in handfuls.

But he was determined to get as far as he could. Perhaps someone would find his body and his diary.

Mawson started walking. His feet felt horribly lumpy and sore. He took off his socks for the first time in days. The soles of his feet had fallen off. He bound the skin back on with bandages and began walking again.

Skiing
Mertz was the Swiss ski-running champion. Skis at this time were heavy and very long. Mertz's skis weighed 11 lbs.

Reducing weight
After Mertz's death, Mawson sawed their sled in half with a penknife so that it was less heavy to pull along.

Six days later, Mawson felt a sickening lurch as he fell into a crevasse. This is the end, he thought. Any moment, the sled would crash onto his head and he would fall into the icy depths.

But suddenly the rope tying him to his sled tightened, as the sled caught in the snow above. Mawson hung inside the crevasse. He began hauling himself up the rope, resting, making another effort, getting closer, till finally he was at the top.

Then the edge of the crevasse collapsed under his weight, and he plummeted down again. Mawson swung, like meat on a butcher's hook. He had tried, and failed. He didn't have the strength to try again. It would be a relief to die.

Yet somehow, Mawson found the will for one last effort. His hands were stiff, his body chilling. In a few moments it would be too late.

Bit by bit Mawson got himself up the rope, and with a superhuman effort swung his legs over the edge, then lay unconscious on the snow.

Ice axe
Explorers usually pull themselves up a steep ice face using two ice axes. Mawson's ice axe fell into the crevasse with Ninnis.

Getting a grip
The ice was dangerously slippery, so Mawson pushed nails and screws into pieces of wood and tied them to his boots to give better grip.

Somehow, Mawson crawled into his sleeping bag. Going on seemed impossible. How much better to lie here, sleep, eat his remaining food, and feel happy, at least for a while.

But then he had an idea. He made a ladder out of rope, tied one end to the sled, and hooked the other over his shoulder. Now he had something to help him survive.

He could scramble up the ladder if he fell into a crevasse – if the sled didn't fall in as well.

Mawson kept going. He reached a food depot called Aladdin's Cave, but was trapped there by bad weather for a week.

Finally he arrived back at the base hut – just six hours after the ship which was due to take everyone home had left. Mawson had to spend the long winter in Antarctica, slowly recovering from his terrible ordeal.

Many years later, doctors found the cause of the mysterious illness that killed Mertz, and affected Mawson so badly. Mawson and Mertz knew that they needed fresh meat to stay healthy, so they had eaten the dogs. But dogs' livers contain lots of Vitamin A, and this had poisoned them. ❖

Cape Denison
Mawson's base was at Cape Denison, on the coast of Adélie Land. It turned out to be the windiest part of Antarctica.

The base hut
The men built two huts, joined together. They slept, cooked and ate in one hut. The second was a workshop.

Terrible winds
The wind was so strong that the men sometimes had to crawl along the ground to avoid being picked up and hurled along.

The *Endurance* sinks

Ernest Shackleton
Irish-born Shackleton first went to Antarctica with Scott in 1901. In 1909 he led an expedition that almost reached the South Pole. In 1914 he set out in his ship, the *Endurance*, aiming to be the first person to walk across Antarctica.

Shackleton's route
Shackleton planned to sail through the icy Weddell Sea and land on the Antarctic coast. He and a party of men would then walk to the South Pole, and across to the other side of Antarctica.

The beginning of the end came on Sunday, October 24, 1916, just after dinner. The *Endurance* lost the fight.

For 278 days the wooden ship had been stuck fast in the dangerous pack ice of the Weddell Sea.

Now three huge ice floes were pressing relentlessly around the ship. The *Endurance* groaned and quivered.

Suddenly, there was a terrible crash! Twisted and fatally bent, the *Endurance* began to let in water.

The men pumped water out until they were exhausted. But still the ice floes pressed in, twisting and grinding with a dreadful roaring noise. The ship's timbers cracked and splintered under the pressure.

Pack ice
The sea around Antarctica is full of pieces of floating ice, called pack ice. It is made of frozen sea water and pieces of ice from the land.

Ice floes
An ice floe is a large sheet of floating sea ice, made of frozen sea water.

Soccer on ice
While the *Endurance* was trapped, the men played soccer on the ice floes.

Ice breaker
Today a specially built ship called an ice breaker can cut a channel through the pack ice.
It leans its bow on the ice and breaks through.

Photos from the *Endurance*
Frank Hurley, the expedition's photographer, rescued his camera and negatives from the ship. His photos give an amazing record of their adventure.

The end came on Wednesday. The *Endurance* was being crushed. It was sickening to feel the decks breaking up and the ship's great wooden beams bending, then snapping with a noise like gunfire.

Frank Hurley took this photo of the Endurance *trapped in the ice.*

The ship's stern lifted 20 feet into the air, the rudder tore off, and water rushed forward and froze, weighing down the bow. The icy black sea poured in.

Ernest Shackleton looked down into the engine room and saw the engines dropping sideways. He gave the order: abandon ship!

The men tumbled out onto the ice, shocked and exhausted. They were standing on a shaking ice floe, just 2 feet thick, floating on the surface of the deep, dark ocean.

That night they camped on the ice. All around them the ice floes groaned and crashed. Three times the ice started splitting and smashing underneath them, and they had to move their tents.

Shackleton decided that they had to walk across the pack ice to reach land. But the land he was aiming for was 312 miles away.

Banjo
One of the men managed to save his banjo. He entertained the others by playing while they sang.

Windproof hood
Shackleton wore this hood when he tried to reach the South Pole in 1909.

Camping on the ice
The men slept, ate, smoked, read, and relaxed in their tents. There wasn't much to do as they drifted on the ice for month after month.

The *James Caird*
The men rescued three lifeboats from the *Endurance*. The largest, the *James Caird*, was only 23 ft long.

They set out on Saturday, dragging food, equipment, and the lifeboats from the *Endurance* over the ice. But in three days, they traveled less than 2 miles.

Shackelton decided they had to stop and camp on the ice. The ice would drift north, taking them nearer to land and safety.

In a way, the ice was friendly. It was solid underfoot. It gave them water to drink. Seals and penguins used the ice, so there would be food to catch.

They chose a large, thick floe for "Ocean Camp." They could still see the *Endurance* in the distance. Parties of men salvaged what they could from the crushed wreck.

One evening, Shackleton saw the *Endurance* begin to sink. "She's going, boys!" he shouted sadly. The men ran to watch. Their ship upended, bow first, and sank slowly under the ice.

The *Endurance* had been their home for so long. She was their last link with the outside world. They felt very lonely now.

Weddell seal
Weddell seals are one of the species of seal that live in the seas around Antarctica.
In spring, the females come up on to the ice to give birth to their pups.

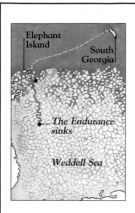

The route to South Georgia
The men floated north through the Weddell Sea on ice floes, then sailed to Elephant Island. There, Shackleton set out in the *James Caird*. He reached South Georgia in May 1916.

Five months later they were still camping. They had drifted slowly north, and now the floes were starting to break up. Their floe heaved and suddenly split. The men crammed into their three lifeboats.

After seven days they managed to reach uninhabited Elephant Island and set up camp on the coast. There, Shackleton left 22 of his men in a small hut.

With five men, he planned to make a dangerous and daring journey. The island of South Georgia lay 800 miles away, across the wild ocean.

They would sail there and get help at one of the whaling stations.

In the little *James Caird*, they made one of the greatest sea journeys ever. After 17 days, they stumbled exhausted on to the shore of South Georgia. But they were on the wrong side of the island.

No one had ever crossed the glaciers and mountains of South Georgia on foot, but Shackleton and two of his men did it to reach help.

It took three months before Shackleton was able to rescue the men on Elephant Island. But everyone who had sailed on the *Endurance* had been saved. ❖

Whaling
Whales were hunted because their bodies could be used to make oil. The bodies were taken to factories called whaling stations to be processed.

South Georgia
This island is mountainous, with glaciers, ice caps, and deep snow.

Locked out in a blizzard!

Richard Byrd
Byrd was an American naval officer and airman. In 1928–30, he led a private expedition to Antarctica and was the navigator on the first flight over the South Pole. On his second expedition in 1933–35, Byrd planned to spend a winter alone at an inland weather station.

Byrd's route
Byrd flew to the inland weather station from his expedition's base camp at Little America. He arrived at the station on March 25, 1934.

Richard Byrd was living in a small wooden hut buried in the ice. Just the roof poked up, with a trapdoor and two ventilator pipes. He was completely on his own.

Byrd had decided to study the Antarctic weather during the winter, far inland. He wanted to be the first person to spend a winter alone, in the interior of Antarctica.

He planned to stay for six months, but after only 60 days he was finding it difficult to say words. He no longer cared how he ate his meals. He ate with his fingers, or out of a can – it didn't matter.

The silence was so enormous that it hurt. The cold was bitter; the darkness unending. He was 123 miles from his base camp, Little America, and he knew that he could not be rescued during the winter.

Byrd often worried about being trapped inside his hut. But one night the opposite happened. He got locked out.

Byrd's hut
The ventilator pipes and the weather equipment were all that showed above ground.

This photo of Byrd in his hut was taken 12 years later, when he went back on a visit.

Weather instruments
Much of Byrd's time was spent recording information from his thermometers and other weather instruments.

Measuring the wind
An instrument called an anemometer measured wind speed and direction.

The temperature outside had dropped to -96°F . A blizzard pounded overhead. One of the weather instruments on the roof broke. Byrd heaved the trapdoor open and crawled out into the screaming wind.

A blinding wall of snow hit him. He couldn't see or hear. He could hardly move. His brains felt as if they were being shaken inside his head. Snow clogged his mouth and nostrils.

Fixing the weather instrument was impossible, so Byrd crawled back to the trapdoor. It was buried in snow. He pulled the handle, but the trapdoor wouldn't budge.

Byrd panicked, clawing and
hitting at the trapdoor. Warmth.
Food. Tools. Everything he needed
to survive was just an arm's length
away, but completely out of reach.
Then his flailing arm hit one
of the metal ventilator pipes.
He peered down it.

Blizzard
Blizzards are
strong winds
that pick up
fine snow lying
on the ground
and hurl it
through the
air. Blizzards
can start in
minutes and
last for days.

Byrd saw a tiny patch of light on
the floor of his hut below. The light
steadied him. Perhaps he could use
the ventilator pipe to lever up the
trapdoor? He tugged, but the pipe
would not budge.

**Byrd's
description**
Byrd wrote that
an Antarctic
blizzard was
"a solid wall
of snow moving
at gale force,
pounding like
surf."

North Pole
Roald Amundsen (left) and Byrd, with the plane in which Byrd flew over the North Pole in 1926.

South Pole
The first flight over the South Pole took place on November 28–29, 1929. Byrd was the navigator.

Famous flag
This American flag was flown from the aircraft as it crossed the South Pole.

Byrd was beginning to lose track of time. He was numbingly cold. Suddenly, he remembered that he'd left a shovel sticking up in the snow a week ago.

He could see nothing, and he didn't dare let go of the pipe or he'd be lost in seconds. He kicked around with his feet, searching for the shovel handle. Nothing. He edged across to the trapdoor and kicked around again. Still nothing.

Desperately, he found the other ventilator pipe and kicked out with his foot. This time his ankle hit something hard – the shovel.

Byrd used the shovel handle as a lever and managed to wrench the trapdoor open at last. He rolled inside and tumbled down into the warmth and light.

The stove had gone out. He didn't care. Byrd pulled off his clothes and fell into bed, exhausted.

Byrd had survived. But just nine days later, he collapsed, poisoned by fumes from his stove and generator.

Byrd was desperately ill, but somehow kept going for over two months, until he could be rescued. He did succeed in spending a winter in the hut, but only just! ❖

Near death
Byrd suffered carbon monoxide poisoning. He was so ill that he could not leave the hut for another two months after the rescue party arrived.

Exploring today

Borge Ousland
Ousland, from Norway, was the first person to reach both the North and South Poles on his own. In 1996 he set out for Antarctica, aiming to be the first person to get across the continent alone, without extra supplies or support.

Anorak
Ousland's anorak was windproof, with many pockets where he could store important things: extra gloves, tape, sun screen, and his compass.

Many explorers tried to cross Antarctica after Shackleton failed in 1915. By the 1990s, one of the last challenges was to cross the continent alone, without support.

Borge Ousland managed to do this, traveling an amazing 1,768 miles across Antarctica in just 64 days.

Ousland was an experienced polar traveler. He trained for the difficult task of pulling his loaded sled by running through the Norwegian forest, dragging three car tires. He cut down every extra bit of weight.

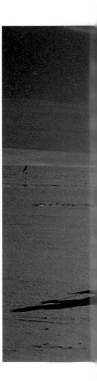

He even sawed his toothbrush in half. He wore the latest lightweight, breathable clothes.

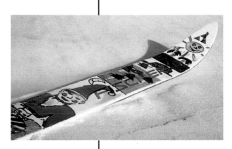

The early explorers wanted to discover the Earth's most southerly continent and its wildlife. Today, scientists study Antarctica, because we now know that what happens there affects the climate, the weather, and the oceans in every part of our planet. ❖

Colorful skis
Ousland's nine-year-old son, Max, painted pictures of pirates, palm trees, and dinosaurs on his skis.
The pictures helped him to keep going.

Ousland traveled on skis, hauling his sled behind him.

Glossary

Antarctica
The huge continent that covers the bottom of the globe. Antarctica is the coldest and windiest place on Earth.

Blizzard
A severe snowstorm. During a blizzard, strong winds pick up fine snow lying on the ground and hurl it through the air.

Base camp
The camp from which an expedition sets out.

Bow
The front part of a ship.

Crevasse
A deep, open crack in the ice of a glacier. It is formed when ice flows over rocks or down a slope and splits apart.

Depot
A place where explorers left supplies of food and fuel to use on their return journey.

Expedition
A group of people who set out on a journey, usually to explore a particular area.

Frostbite
Damage caused to toes, fingers, and other parts of the body when cold conditions make them freeze.

Glacier
A mass of ice which is moving very slowly down mountains or off the land into the sea.

Ice floe
A large sheet of floating sea ice.

Ice breaker
A specially built ship that can break a route through pack ice. It leans its bow on the ice and breaks through.

Iceberg
A large piece of floating ice that has broken off a glacier or ice shelf.

Ice shelf
A large, floating sheet of ice that is permanently attached to land.

Lifeboat
A small boat kept on a bigger ship for use in an emergency.

Man-hauling
Using people to pull a sled. They wear harnesses attached to the sled and drag it along behind them.

Pack ice
Large areas of ice that float in the seas around Antarctica. Pack ice drifts with the ocean currents and the winds.

Pemmican
A food made of dried meat, ground to a powder, and mixed with melted fat.

Polar plateau
The high, flat land in the center of Antarctica that surrounds the South Pole.

Research station
A base where scientists live and study the Antarctic. Many different countries have research stations in Antarctica.

Sled
A low platform on two long runners, shaped like skis. Sleds are used to carry loads over snow and ice.

Sled dogs
Dogs that pull sleds.

Snow bridge
A crust-like lid of snow that often covers the top of a crevasse.

South Pole
The Earth spins around an imaginary line, called its axis. The southernmost end of this line is the South Pole.

Stern
The back part of a ship.

Whaling station
A place where people who hunted whales lived.

Index